WAYS TO MAKE THE WORLD BETTER!

LISA M. GERRY

NATIONAL GEOGRAPHIC KiDS

WASHINGTON, D.C.

Sure, they might not be old enough to vote. Most of them can't drive. And many of them aren't tall enough for all the rides at the amusement park. **But one thing is for sure when it comes to kids—they are natural activists.** They take risks and they build bridges. And they instinctively recognize fairness. **In big ways and small, they have changed the history of the world.**

In 1963, a group of young people changed the course of the **U.S. civil rights movement** to end racial discrimination and segregation against African Americans in the United States. **Thousands of kids—some only eight years old—hit the streets of Birmingham, Alabama.** The children were arrested, hit with crushing blasts from fire hoses, and threatened by police dogs. As the days passed, the kids stuck to their **nonviolent training.** They sang protest songs together and held firm. The fight for civil rights continued for years, but this demonstration marked a significant shift in the momentum of the movement. The media attention these protests received made it **impossible** for people around the country—**and around the world—to ignore the injustice that was taking place.**

Marley Dias is another great example. When she was 11 years old, Marley asked an important question: **Where are all the books about people of color?** It's a real problem. In 2015, fewer than **10 percent** of children's books published included a black person as a main character. Marley took action. She announced a goal of collecting 1,000 books about black girls, and launched #1000blackgirlbooks. Her efforts went viral, and now **Marley has collected more than 10,000 books.** More important, she has **brought the need for diverse children's books to the world's attention.**

These kids are **extraordinary,** but our future depends on the fact that they are **not unique.**

I am an activist, too—and I was an activist as a kid. Growing up in a small town in Appalachia, I was steeped in stories of the **civil rights movement.** I clearly remember sitting next to my mother in contentious community meetings in support of the **Equal Rights Amendment.** Those early lessons about activism stuck with me. Years later when I was an attorney and volunteered at a Washington, D.C., soup kitchen, I realized that the kids there didn't have any books to read. In response, two friends and I launched a **nonprofit social enterprise called First Book** so that all kids—no matter their current life circumstances—**grow up with books and every other resource required for equal education.** That was 25 years and more than **160 million books ago.** Since then, First Book has become a groundbreaking nonprofit that aims to solve the resource issue PERMANENTLY.

If you are an adult reading this wonderful book, **you already know that every single young person is wired to be a change-maker—and the world needs ALL of them.**

If you are a kid reading this great book, **look in the mirror. What do you see? A curious mind. Sparkly eyes. And a BIG HEART that wants to do something good for the world. Now, take a deep breath and step out.**

This book is designed to help you bring your ideas for positive change into action. **Creating positive change comes in all shapes and sizes.** Wherever and whoever you are, **the world needs you.**

We are all here to help— but you must lead.

KYLE ZIMMER
PRESIDENT, CEO AND
CO-FOUNDER, FIRST BOOK

1 Be open to difFeReNt opinions.

Think about how many people you've met throughout your life. It's a lot, right? And you have a lot of living left to do. Not every person you meet is going to think and feel the same way you do about everything. And that's a good thing! Can you imagine a world where everyone had the same ideas and the same feelings? It'd be pretty boring, right?

SO THE NEXT TIME SOMEONE HAS A DIFFERENT OPINION—SIT BACK AND

HEAR THEM OUT.

It might just open your eyes to a whole new world!

You Can Do It Today!

An anthropologist is someone who studies humans, their cultures, and their social customs. They study people all over the world to find out what makes us different and what makes us the same. Try thinking of yourself as an amateur anthropologist. Ask several people a few questions to find out what makes them tick. Don't tell them they're right or wrong—just listen, with the goal of understanding them better.

Find your voice and RAISE IT.

2

Want to hear something pretty awesome? **You have the power to create change in the world.** In fact, everybody does! The first step toward making a difference is to **find your voice.**

So ... what is "your voice" exactly? It's the unique way you share your own story and the one-of-a-kind ways you express your feelings and ideas and opinions.

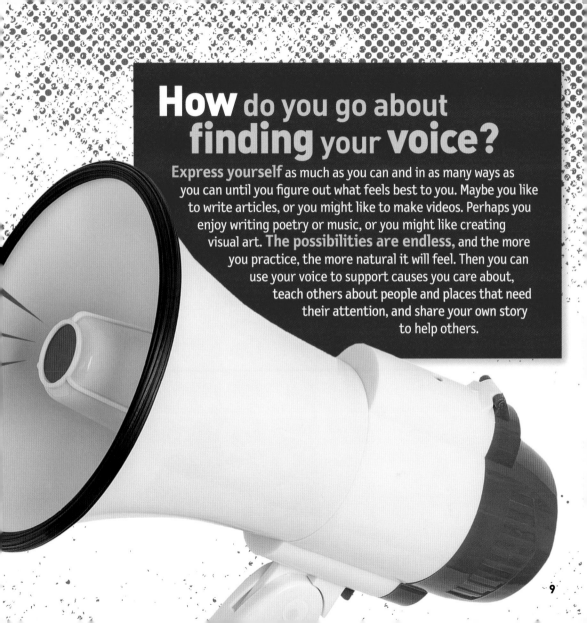

How do you go about finding your voice?

Express yourself as much as you can and in as many ways as you can until you figure out what feels best to you. Maybe you like to write articles, or you might like to make videos. Perhaps you enjoy writing poetry or music, or you might like creating visual art. **The possibilities are endless,** and the more you practice, the more natural it will feel. Then you can use your voice to support causes you care about, teach others about people and places that need their attention, and share your own story to help others.

HISTORY HAS HAIR-RAISING ACTION AND TEAR-JERKING DRAMA. It has heroes and villains. underdog stories, and many, many "I can't believe they did that" moments. It's funny, it's scary, it's amazing, it's sad. **And. It's. ALL. True.** It's history. The story of how we got here.

TIM BAILEY IS A FORMER U.S. HISTORY TEACHER. He taught elementary and middle school students, and was named National History Teacher of the Year in 2009. Today, Tim is director of education at the Gilder Lehrman Institute of American History in New York City. On the next page, he talks about how knowing our past can help make our future better.

What do you love so much about history?

History tells us the story of who we are and how we got here, both personally and as a nation. History isn't just about names and dates and events, history is a story about people. It's individual people, and the choices they make, that change history.

Why is it so important to learn about history?

History shows us where our country's ideals came from and what it took to achieve them. Once you understand why and how certain parts of our government came about, you can make an argument based on evidence and knowledge about whether or not to change things.

How can someone be a better history student?

Learning happens when you make an emotional connection to the subject matter. When you care about something, you retain it. So, find a connection to the stories and try to understand why people did what they did and what motivated them. You might see something in someone that you recognize in yourself, or maybe they remind you of a family member. You don't just have to connect to someone's positive attributes, either, it can also be to their flaws.

Tim's Five Favorites

Favorite Lesson to Teach:

The Declaration of Independence. When the Second Continental Congress decided that the vote for independence had to be unanimous, the probability of that happening with such a diverse group of people seemed so low. It's an amazing story and has such important themes, like compromise and the sacrifice of individuals for the greater good.

Favorite Book:

Killer Angels by Michael Shaara about the Battle of Gettysburg.

Favorite Movie:

Glory is a great movie about the Civil War and the important, and often ignored, role that African-American soldiers played in it.

Favorite Quote:

"The important thing is not to stop questioning. Curiosity has its own reason for existing."
—Albert Einstein

Favorite Historical Figure:

One of my favorites is Abigail Adams, who was the wife of John Adams, the second U.S. president. She stood up in a man's world and said, *Hello! Really? Come on!* She was such a strong individual.

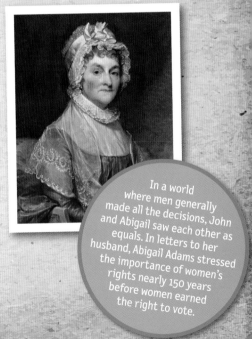

In a world where men generally made all the decisions, John and Abigail saw each other as equals. In letters to her husband, Abigail Adams stressed the importance of women's rights nearly 150 years before women earned the right to vote.

Spend time with OLDER individuals.

Call your grandparents, visit a senior living facility, or stop by a neighbor's house to sit down and chat. It will make them **happy,** and it will make you feel **good. A bonus?** They have awesome stories to share.

BY NOW, YOU PROBABLY ALREADY KNOW THAT YOU SHOULD RECYCLE, BUT DO YOU KNOW WHY?

HERE ARE A FEW GREAT REASONS:

- Americans make more than **200 million tons** (181 t) of garbage each year. That's a lot. And unless we want our Earth covered in trash, we have to start sending less of it to landfills. Recycling does that!

- Because new things are being made from already existing items, recycling means there's less need to use more natural resources like wood, water, and minerals.

- Recycling prevents pollution and saves energy.

  - Recycling reduces greenhouse gas emissions, which contribute to climate change.

FUN FACT!

Recycling **ONE SODA CAN** saves enough **ENERGY** to listen to a **FULL** album on your mp3 player.

STAND UP FOR JUSTICE.

Have you ever gotten into trouble for something you didn't do? Then you've experienced **injustice,** or **something that is unfair.** Injustice happens every day, in small ways, and in big ways, like when **entire groups of people** are treated **unfairly** or **unequally** due to things like their gender, race, or religion.

It takes real **courage** to **speak up** when you see injustice, when that little voice inside you says, **"Hey, that's not right."** So, if you see someone being **picked on** or treated like they're different or less than other people, find a **safe way** to **say or do** something. That might mean speaking to a teacher, coach, parent, or school counselor. Or it might mean saying to whoever's being mistreated, **"I'm sorry that happened. You didn't deserve it. I support you."**

66 Total Quotable 99

"Injustice anywhere is a threat to justice everywhere."
—Martin Luther King, Jr.

speak up!

stand up!

BE fair

JUSTICE for all!

SAY something

Be nice to yourself.

7

After all, you're with you 24 hours a day. You know your hopes, fears, and dreams better than anyone else. And like it or not, you're stuck with you for the rest of your life.

The way you treat yourself matters a lot. It affects your ability to do great things. And the kindness you show yourself will ripple out into the world and make it a better place.

20

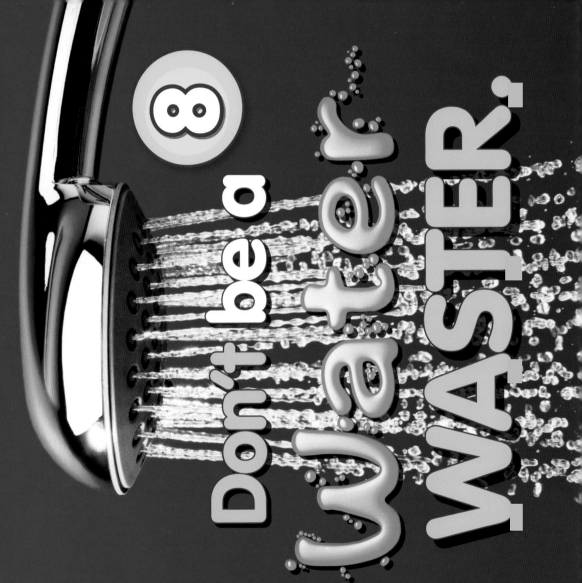

8

Don't be a Water WASTER.

One in 10 people in the world doesn't have access to clean drinking water. It's important to remember that our clean water doesn't come without a price to the environment. It takes a lot of energy to treat and heat the water that comes out of the faucets in our homes. By cutting down on the amount of water we use, we can help the environment in a major way!

HERE ARE FIVE WAYS TO BE AN H2O HERO:

1. Don't let the faucet run while you're brushing your teeth.

2. Cut your shower time in half. (The average American family uses 40 gallons [151 L] of water per day for showers!)

3. When washing the car, use a bucket instead of letting the hose run.

4. Only run machines that use water, like the dishwasher and the washing machine, when you have a full load.

5. Be a drip detective and point out any water leaks to your parents. Faucet, shower, and toilet leaks are a huge contributor to water waste.

Dream **BIG.**

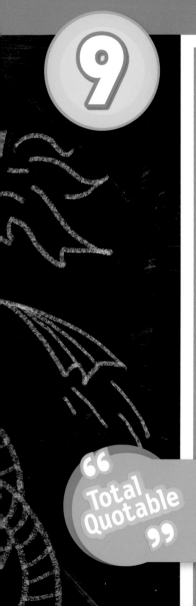

9

Set aside time to let your mind wander, to let yourself wonder *What if?*, and to let yourself dream. Because dreaming leads to big ideas. And big ideas have the power to change the world. Big ideas lead to discoveries that help people who are sick. Big ideas lead to inventions that save our environment. Big ideas inspire books, TV shows, movies, and music that make people happy and make people think. There is no limit to what big ideas can do. And there is no limit to what you can do, so long as you keep having BIG IDEAS.

Total Quotable

"Every great dream begins with a dreamer. Always remember, you have within you the strength, the patience, and the passion to reach for the stars to change the world."
—Harriet Tubman

Practice **positive** **body** image.

10

Think about everything you can do. Can you **pet a puppy? Eat a cookie? Feel the wind in your hair** when you step outside? Yes, yes, and yes? **Well ... you have your body to thank for that.**

Maybe there are things you wish you could change about your body. Maybe you wish you were a little bit **taller** or **shorter. Bigger** or **smaller.** Had straighter teeth or skin that was lighter or darker. But it's the body you were born with. And guess what? **It's incredible.**

Think of your body as a shell that holds all your **best** parts: your brain and heart, funny quirks, and so on. And other people's bodies are like shells that hold the best of them.

So don't bad-mouth your bod—or anyone else's. And if you ever need a reminder of why it's so great, just take this quiz!

PRACTICE POSITIVE BODY IMAGE.

The "Everybody's Body Is Amazing" Quiz

Not feeling super comfortable in your own skin? Grab a piece of paper and jot down your answers to these questions. Sometimes reminding yourself how phenomenal your body is makes all the difference!

1 WHAT IS YOUR *FAVORITE* PART OF YOUR BODY? WHY?

2 WHAT'S SOMETHING *UNIQUE* ABOUT YOUR BODY?

3 WHAT'S ONE OF YOUR *FAVORITE* THINGS TO DO OR PLAY? **HOW** DOES YOUR **BODY HELP** YOU DO THAT?

4 WHAT'S SOMETHING YOU *CAN DO* THIS YEAR THAT YOU *COULDN'T* DO LAST YEAR? **HOW** DID YOUR **BODY HELP** YOU ACHIEVE **THIS?**

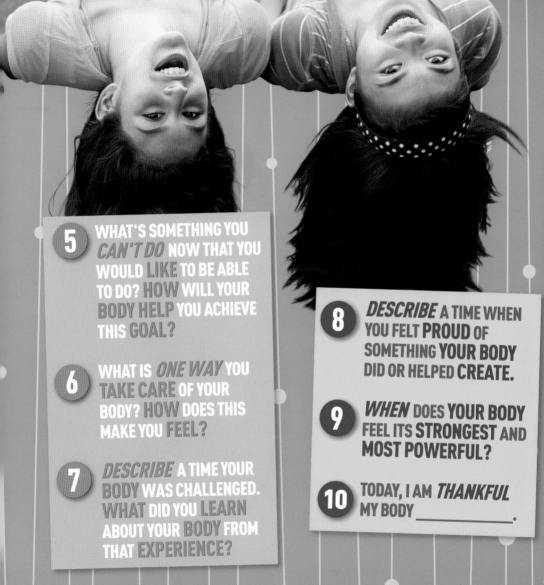

5 WHAT'S SOMETHING YOU *CAN'T DO* NOW THAT YOU WOULD LIKE TO BE ABLE TO DO? HOW WILL YOUR BODY HELP YOU ACHIEVE THIS GOAL?

6 WHAT IS *ONE WAY* YOU TAKE CARE OF YOUR BODY? HOW DOES THIS MAKE YOU FEEL?

7 *DESCRIBE* A TIME YOUR BODY WAS CHALLENGED. WHAT DID YOU LEARN ABOUT YOUR BODY FROM THAT EXPERIENCE?

8 *DESCRIBE* A TIME WHEN YOU FELT PROUD OF SOMETHING YOUR BODY DID OR HELPED CREATE.

9 *WHEN* DOES YOUR BODY FEEL ITS STRONGEST AND MOST POWERFUL?

10 TODAY, I AM *THANKFUL* MY BODY _____.

11

Don't let your fears hold you back.

Hannah Reyes Morales is a **photographer** living in the Philippines. She is a **National Geographic Young Explorer,** photographing people whose lives she's curious about. "Without photography, perhaps I never would have been able to **connect** with some of my subjects, **ask** them questions, or **observe** the way they live their lives," says Hannah. "I hope that my work exposes people to places and ways of life they **haven't seen before,** and maybe even **inspires** them to **care a little more** about the world."

Here Hannah talks about **facing her fears** and how **bravery** can make the world a better place.

Where did you grow up? What was your life like there?

I grew up very simply, in Manila. I was an only child, with a single mom. But we were always surrounded by other family members. In fact, there were 12 other people who lived in our house.

What made you want to become a photographer?

Growing up, I didn't know much outside of the room I shared with my mom, so when I found photography I started dreaming about exploring other places. I read my mom's *National Geographic* and *LIFE* magazines, and the photographs captured my imagination. I read about the lives of photographers in the field, and as a young girl, I got very excited about seeing new things and learning about other cultures.

Has there been a time in your career that you had to face a fear?

I face fear at work constantly. Even if I am very excited about a job, there's often a big part of me that has many fears, and I have to face them all the time. I've gotten lost in places where I didn't speak the language, swam with whale sharks in the open ocean, climbed up to frightening heights, gone to a volcano's crater, and been in the middle of violent demonstrations. In facing my fears, I try to remember that I have done my best to prepare for these situations, and I remind myself that I have the right tools to face them.

"After facing my fears, I always find that I have learned something new—and that helps me face other challenges."

How do you think facing a fear can help make the world a better place?

Being brave makes the world a better place. It helps us do the right thing when faced with the choice to do something, or to do nothing instead. For example, when we face our fears, we're better equipped to stand up to an intimidating bully and show kindness to those who need it, even when we don't have to. In facing our fears, we can satisfy our curiosity, attempt our dreams, and reach out to people whose voices are not heard.

What else has your work taught you?

My work has taught me to try again after I fail at something. It has shown me that I am capable of doing more than I thought I could do, and it has helped me discover and develop strengths that I never thought I had. The truth is, I am actually scared of many things, and growing up I never thought I could be brave. But through my work, I have become courageous, and I have done things that I hadn't thought were possible.

Have FUN!

Even when the going gets tough, always remember to have fun. **Laugh, play, dance, sing** ... do what makes you happy. **Happiness** is contagious, after all.

THINK
about things
CRITICALLY.

13

Being a CRITICAL THINKER means that BEFORE you believe something or someone, you CONSIDER THE FACTS AND EVIDENCE. For example, take something you might read on the Internet. MOST of the information you find there is definitely not fact-checked. So you have to become your own info investigator. DOUBLE-CHECK! FIND ANOTHER RELIABLE SOURCE THAT CAN VERIFY, OR CONFIRM, THE INFORMATION.

When trying to determine whether or not to trust a source, or the information provided, consider these questions:

Who is this information coming from? Who is the original source?

Is this source reliable? Why or why not?

Does this source have an agenda or a motive for sharing this information?

What does this source gain from me believing this information?

Do other reliable sources confirm or agree with this information?

37

TURN
OFF THE
LIGHTS
**WHEN YOU
LEAVE
THE ROOM.**

14

Weird but true!

Almost 50 percent of devices and electronics—like TVs, laptops, and washing machines—use energy even when they're turned off. So, in some cases, the only way to stop an appliance from using energy is to unplug it.

15

HELP someone OUT.

If you see your teacher struggling to put books away, jump up and help! Then ask if there's anything else you can do. Check in with elderly neighbors to see if they'd like a hand shoveling snow or bringing their garbage cans in. See someone with an armload of groceries? Offer to carry something or to hold a door. Helping is sort of like exercising a muscle—the more you do it, the easier it is and the better it feels.

Total Quotable

66

"When I was a boy and I would see scary things in the news, my mother would say to me, 'Look for the helpers. You will always find people who are helping.'" —Mr. Fred Rogers

99

41

Practice Gratitude.

We all have bad moods, and we all have bad days. The thing is, try as we may, we can't control a lot of what happens to us. But what we can control is how we think about what happens to us and how we react to it. One of the quickest ways to fight off a funk, brush off a bad mood, and begin to see the bright side is by practicing gratitude.

⑯ PRACTICE GRATITUDE.

Gratitude means appreciating and being thankful for all the stuff that's good. So, sure, it might be raining, and you may have gotten mud on your brand-new shoes. But when you practice gratitude, instead of letting that ruin your day, you might sit for a minute and think about how thankful you are to have brand-new shoes and how much you appreciate that you have someone who would probably help you clean them if you want. Then you might think about a few more things you're grateful for—like it being Pizza Day in the cafeteria, that you finally got rid of that annoying cold, that your dog learned to roll over, your warm bed, and your awesome friends!

On any given day, no matter how much not-so-good stuff is going on, if you really look for it, you'll find a lot to be grateful for.

And studies have shown that just the act of practicing gratitude—like writing down three things you're thankful for each day—comes with tons of benefits, including improved physical health, less anxiety, better sleep, and more friends!

"The single greatest thing you can do to change your life today would be to start being grateful for what you have right now." —Oprah Winfrey

Total Quotable

So why not start now?

What are **three things** you're grateful for today?

Trust your
INTUITION.

You know that **little voice inside of you** that says things like, "Ummm, I don't think I should take a shortcut through this alley," or "Hey, maybe I should apologize, I think I hurt her feelings," or perhaps, "I have a feeling this person isn't telling the truth." **That's your intuition.** It's kind of like your **antennae.** It helps you feel out a situation to get a sense of **what's really going on,** beyond the obvious, below the surface.

Your intuition is a super valuable resource. It can **protect** you from danger, **lead** you to awesome opportunities, or give you a **heads-up** when things might not be as they seem. But the key to success when it comes to your intuition is **recognizing it** and **paying attention** to it.

So when you get a **feeling in your gut,** or when you **hear that little voice—** and it may be a whisper or a scream— **listen to it.**

47

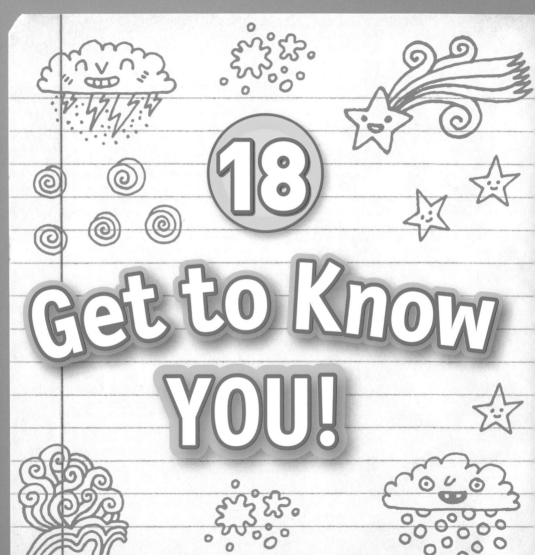

18 Get to Know YOU!

You may be thinking, *What? I already know me! I am myself, after all.* Well, that's true. But have you ever taken the time to really sit down and **think** about who you truly are? What you really like and dislike? How you really **feel** about things? By being your **authentic self**, you'll not only fill the you-shaped hole in the world, you'll also **inspire** other people to be themselves, which, if you think about it, is pretty cool.

So who are YOU exactly? This quiz will get you started on your quest.

The "Getting to Know You" Quiz

1 What is something that always makes you smile?

2 Name three times when you were really, really happy.

3 Who or what makes you laugh the hardest?

4 What's something that makes you angry?

5 What's something that gets you fired up?

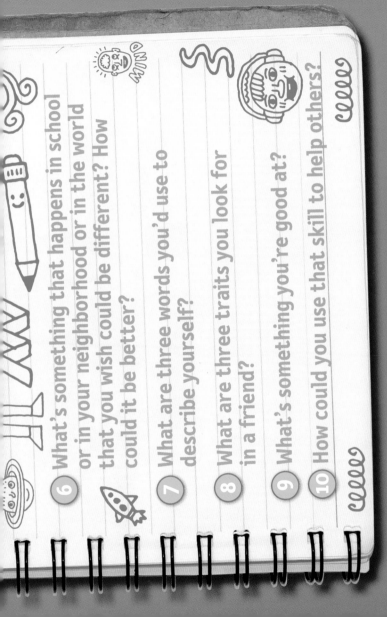

6 What's something that happens in school or in your neighborhood or in the world that you wish could be different? How could it be better?

7 What are three words you'd use to describe yourself?

8 What are three traits you look for in a friend?

9 What's something you're good at?

10 How could you use that skill to help others?

Total Quotable

"Be yourself. Everyone else is already taken."

—Oscar Wilde

TAKE ACTION.

WILL

MATTY

All right, so something has you **FIRED UP,** you're **FEELING ALL THE FEELS,** and you are **READY AND RARIN' TO GO** to help make the world a better place. Now what? The next step is to find a way to use your feelings and your ideas to **DO** something.

That's exactly what **WILL GLADSTONE,** a 12-year-old from Massachusetts, U.S.A., did when he learned that the **BLUE-FOOTED BOOBY** was at risk of becoming **ENDANGERED.** Together with his younger brother Matty, he started **THE BLUE FEET FOUNDATION,** which sells **BRIGHT BLUE SOCKS** to raise money to help the birds.

When did you first learn about the blue-footed booby? What do you like about them or find most interesting?

In the fifth grade, we did a big bird project. The blue-footed booby was one of the ones we learned about. They stood out to me because they dance and have bright blue feet. They're quirky, and I had never seen a bird like it before.

What made you decide you wanted to do something to help?

It made me sad that they might go extinct. I want everyone to be able to see one.

How did you come up with the idea to sell socks to help raise money for them?

There was a poster of birds on the wall in my science class, and I saw the blue-footed booby. Then I looked down at my feet, and it just hit me: *I could sell blue socks to raise money for the bird that has blue feet! It would be so cool if everyone could have blue feet.*

How did you know you would be able to help?

I figured any money we made would be better than no money. I contacted a bunch of charities, but none of them took Matty—who's nine—and me seriously because we were kids. When I emailed the Galápagos Conservancy, they replied that they would take our donations. They protect the Galápagos Islands, which is where the blue-footed boobies live. Having them believe in us gave us confidence.

How much money have you raised for the blue-footed booby so far? How many pairs of socks have you sold?

We've raised $15,000 so far, and we've sold 1,600 pairs. We've had orders from 46 states and 14 countries. It's really cool getting orders from around the world. People send us pictures of them wearing the socks, and that's cool, too.

"Never doubt that a small group of thoughtful committed citizens can change the world; indeed, it's the only thing that ever has."
—Margaret Mead

Total Quotable

What have you learned from starting this business?

I've learned it can be really hard. Every day when we come home from school, I pack up and ship the new orders. I also update our Instagram account with a photo someone sent us or a cool fact about the blue-footed booby. It's a big commitment, and now that I'm really helping the bird, I can't stop. But it's really fun! I like getting pictures, seeing that the socks make people happy, and knowing that I'm really helping the blue-footed booby. I also like working with my brother. Another thing I've learned is that if I have an idea that I believe in, I can really make it happen— even if adults don't like it.

What advice would you give other young people who want to make a difference?

I'd tell them to find something they really care about. If they want to be successful, they're going to have to spend a lot of time doing it. We weren't successful in the beginning. Once we got the socks and had our website up, it was almost the whole summer before we got an order. We had to try a lot of different things to get people to notice our socks. If we had quit after a few months, we never would have been success-ful. You have to try a lot of things before you know what works. You can't give up.

LISTEN. 20

Every person has a story. It might be a story about their past. It could be about their hopes and their dreams for their future. Their story could be about their fears or what makes them sad. Or it could be about what makes their soul sing. But no matter what words they use when they share their story—what they're really telling you is who they are.

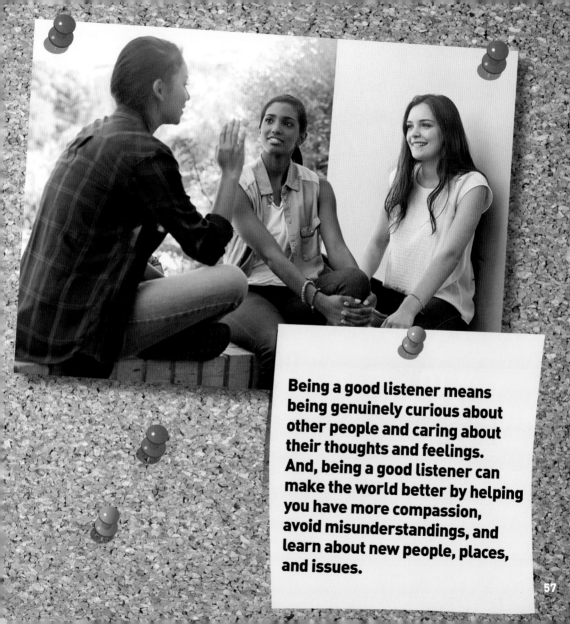

Being a good listener means being genuinely curious about other people and caring about their thoughts and feelings. And, being a good listener can make the world better by helping you have more compassion, avoid misunderstandings, and learn about new people, places, and issues.

HERE ARE *FIVE WAYS* YOU CAN *BOOST* YOUR *LISTENING* SKILLS.

FOCUS.
That means putting away all distractions and really giving whoever's talking your full attention.

DON'T INTERRUPT.
This might seem pretty obvious, but it can be very difficult for some people to put into practice. Give whoever's talking the space and the time to express themselves the way they want to. If someone's sharing, don't cut them off, don't try to guess and fill in what they're trying to say, and don't bring the subject back to you by saying something like, "Well I know when that happened to me ..." Just relax and breathe and listen.

TRY TO UNDERSTAND.
Don't worry too much about having a response ready when the person stops talking. Instead, really try to figure out what it is they're trying to say.

BE OPEN-MINDED.

When someone is telling you something personal, they're trusting you with their truth. They're giving you a little glimpse into their heart and their mind. So be respectful of that and try not to rush to judgment.

LET THEM KNOW THAT YOU UNDERSTAND (OR THAT MAYBE YOU DON'T).

When you want to make sure someone knows you're hearing them, you can say something like, "It sounds like what you're saying is ..." or "Do you mean ...?" Or, if you don't understand and you need them to clarify, you can say something like, "I really want to understand, could you say that a different way?" Or, "I think I understand, but I want to be sure, do you mean ...?"

" Total Quotable **"**

"We have two ears and one mouth so that we can listen twice as much as we speak."
—Epictetus

21

think BALLY.

GLOBALLY

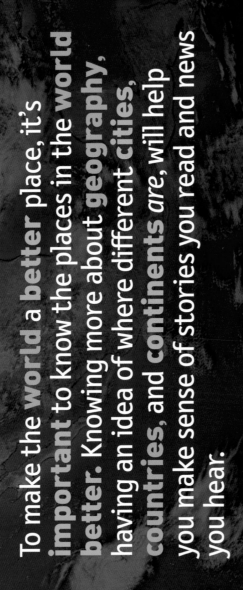

To make the world a better place, it's important to know the places in the world better. Knowing more about geography, having an idea of where different cities, countries, and continents *are*, will help you make sense of stories you read and news you hear.

When you hear about a new place, make a habit of looking for it on a map. See what continent it's on, what big cities are nearby, and if it's close to a body of water. Then look up what language or languages are spoken there, some of the most popular foods or dishes eaten there, and popular modes of transportation. Getting a sense of the people who live there, and what daily life might be like for them, will help make that place more than a dot on a map in your mind.

FEELING WORLDLY? TRY YOUR HAND AT **A FEW** QUESTIONS **FROM PAST** NATIONAL GEOGRAPHIC GEOGRAPHY BEES.

Q: Did you know that whales have belly buttons? It's true! Several species of whales live in the Weddell Sea near the Ronne [ROH-nuh] Ice Shelf on which continent?

A: Antarctica

Q: It might be hard to believe, but there is cell phone reception at the summit of Mount Everest. This mountain, the highest on Earth, is located in the Himalaya on which continent?

A: Asia

Q: The city of Amsterdam, in the Netherlands, has more bikes than people. Wild, huh? This city is located near the North Sea on which continent?

A: Europe

Q: Red diamonds are some of the rarest stones in the world. These diamonds are mined on which continent that borders the Coral and Timor Seas?

A: Australia

Q: An ostrich's eye is bigger than its brain. This bird can be found in the Kalahari and Namib Deserts on which continent?

A: Africa

22

Let your TRASH be someone else's TREASURE.

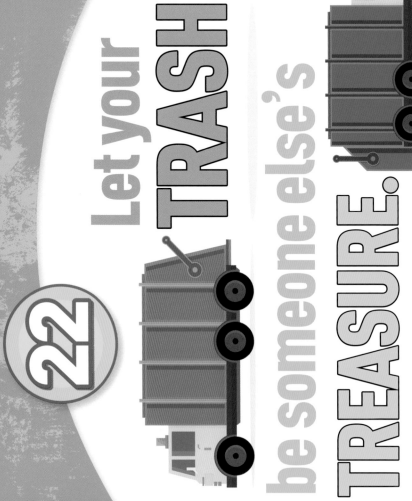

Are your old soccer cleats too small? Are the toys you played with two years ago losing their luster? Did you get a new sleeping bag to replace the old one with the tiny hole? Well, before you send all of your old stuff to the landfill by way of the trash can, consider donating it instead.

Cutting down on your clutter? Check! Sending less trash to landfills? Check! Helping someone in need? Check! If you think about it, donating is really the ultimate win-win-win!

Your things will either be resold at a discounted rate (and hey, someone else might really need that discount right now!) or be recycled. For instance, clothes that are too stained or torn are sometimes cut up and used as insulation, carpet padding, or industrial rags.

WHAT IS A LANDFILL?

If you've ever been on a long road trip, chances are you've passed landfills. They look like large, long, flat-topped hills on the side of the road, and usually there are lots of birds hovering above them. But the real giveaway is the smell. Landfills smell funk-ay.

Landfills are one of the oldest waste management strategies and still the most popular in the United States. Basically, a hole is cut into the ground, a plastic layer is placed in the hole to try to keep the waste from coming into contact with the groundwater, and then all the trash people throw away is put into the hole. The pile of trash is then covered with soil so that the solid waste doesn't come into contact with the air or rain.

The thing is, some stuff people throw away has toxic chemicals in it. And sometimes these toxic chemicals do come into contact with the soil and the groundwater, which then goes into the earth or nearby bodies of water. Also, as certain materials decompose in landfills, methane gas, a greenhouse gas that contributes to climate change, is released.

When you understand what a landfill is, and certainly when you see one, it makes sense that we should try to reduce the need for more landfills. How do we do that? By making less trash and recycling.

23

TAKE UP A COLLECTION.

Raise money for a cause you care about. You could hold a **car wash**, auction off a service like **babysitting** or **baking**, use an online crowdfunding site, or just place containers for spare change around the school.

69

24 Be a welcoming committee!

It can be pretty nerve-wracking moving to a new place. New kids in town might not have any friends yet; they might not know their way around; and they won't know the cool lingo—they may not even know the language.

Often, all it takes to make it better is one kind person who smiles at them, offers to show them around, and says, "Hey, you can sit with me." That person has the power to make a big difference in someone's life. And you know what? That person could be YOU.

25

Write a *thank-you*
note to someone who's not expecting it.

Be *specific,*
be *honest,*
be *heartfelt,*
and let the
person know
what his or
her actions
meant to you.

73

Notice something that needs to be taken care of, and do it **before** you're asked.

27

Spend time reading with someone younger.

28

BE generous with COMPLIMENTS.

IF YOU'RE THINKING SOMETHING NICE ABOUT SOMEONE, TELL THEM!

You'll make their day. You'll feel WONDERFUL. And, since kindness is contagious, chances are they'll pay it forward and give someone else a compliment, keeping the good vibes flowing.

79

29
Plant a tree.

Besides being beautiful, attracting birds and butterflies, and creating the perfect shady spot to sit and read or draw, trees can help the environment in a major way. Through the process of photosynthesis, trees absorb carbon dioxide—a greenhouse gas that contributes to climate change—and other pollutants in the atmosphere.

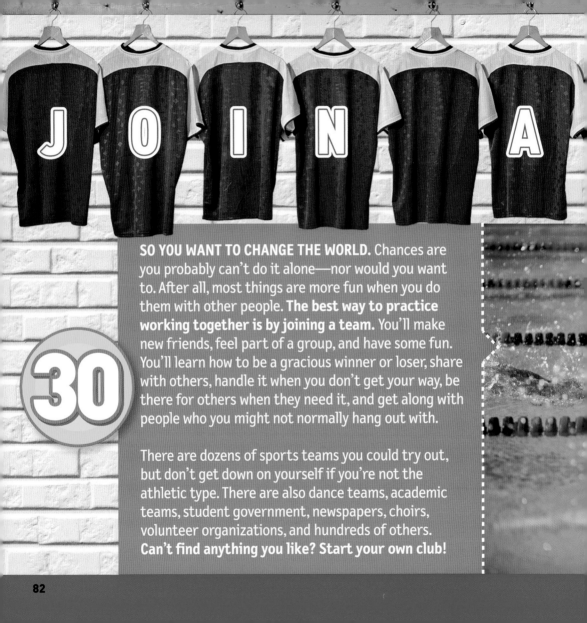

JOIN A

SO YOU WANT TO CHANGE THE WORLD. Chances are you probably can't do it alone—nor would you want to. After all, most things are more fun when you do them with other people. **The best way to practice working together is by joining a team.** You'll make new friends, feel part of a group, and have some fun. You'll learn how to be a gracious winner or loser, share with others, handle it when you don't get your way, be there for others when they need it, and get along with people who you might not normally hang out with.

There are dozens of sports teams you could try out, but don't get down on yourself if you're not the athletic type. There are also dance teams, academic teams, student government, newspapers, choirs, volunteer organizations, and hundreds of others. **Can't find anything you like? Start your own club!**

30

TEAM.

Learn another LANGUAGE.

31

You'll find that it's **REALLY THRILLING** to be able to **COMMUNICATE** with someone in a **DIFFERENT LANGUAGE;** you'll learn a lot about other **CULTURES;** and it means **SO MUCH** to people when you learn the language they speak.

How to say "HELLO" in 10 languages

GERMAN:
Guten Tag

FARSI:
Salaam

PORTUGUESE:
Oi

SPANISH:
Hola

MANDARIN:
Nǐ Hǎo

ARABIC:
Marhabaan

HINDI:
Namaste

SWAHILI:
Jambo

ITALIAN:
Ciao

FRENCH:
Bonjour

32

OWN UP TO YOUR **MISTAKES.**

IT'S INEVITABLE: At some point in your life, you will **mess up. And there's no shame in that.** But HOW you handle the mistake afterward says a lot about **who you are.** It makes sense that your first instinct might be to hide the necklace you broke or pretend your retainer got stolen (when really you threw it away with your lunch tray), but one of the quickest ways to earn the respect of others is to **admit** when you mess up. It takes real strength and integrity to stand up and say, "I made a mistake. I'm sorry. Here's how I'm going to try to make it right." People respect honesty, and hey, you might even get off easier in return!

33

PUT YOUR TALENTS TO USE.

EVERYBODY'S GOOD AT *SOMETHING.* ONCE YOU FIGURE OUT WHAT YOUR SOMETHING IS, PUT IT TO **GOOD USE** HELPING PEOPLE.

DO YOU LIKE TO SING?
Head over to the local retirement community and put on a concert.

ARE YOU GREAT WITH KIDS?
Offer to assist with the children at a women's shelter, at your church, or for a family in your neighborhood who needs a little extra help.

CAN YOU KNIT?
Whip up some hats and scarves and donate them to a local homeless shelter.

ARE YOU CRAZY FOR CRAFTING? Make someone a homemade card or picture frame to brighten their day!

ARE YOU KIND OF KILLING IT IN ONE OF YOUR CLASSES? Offer to be a study buddy for someone who's struggling with that subject.

ARE YOU GREAT WITH ANIMALS? Volunteer at an animal shelter or offer to help a neighbor who's just had surgery by walking their dog.

ARE YOU A GOOD COOK OR BAKER? Make some food or treats for someone going through a rough time.

REMEMBER, YOU, RIGHT NOW, *JUST AS YOU ARE,* HAVE THE **POWER** TO HELP OTHER PEOPLE. START BY THINKING OF **YOUR OWN GIFTS** AND HOW **YOU** MIGHT **SHARE** THEM.

Total Quotable

"We can't help everyone, but everyone can help someone."
—Ronald Reagan

34

TEACH
someone
how to do
something
you know how to
DO WELL.

35

Disconnect from your electronics.

One of the most **powerful** ways to make your life and the lives of others **better** is by **socializing.** Sure, you can do that by texting or posting on social networks, but the big benefits come from **interacting** the old-fashioned way—IRL, like face-to-face. (Though that excuse might not hold up when you get into trouble for chatting in class.)

So **leave your phone at home** (or at least in your pocket) today, and **be present.** Make it your mission to smile and say "Hi" to the people you encounter. If there's a moment when you're alone or bored, instead of reaching for a device, let your mind wander. Notice your surroundings. Then at the end of the day, ask yourself how you feel. Did you have any **nice interactions** with people? Did you notice any **cool/ fun/funny** details you wouldn't have had you been looking down?

FUN FACT!

Studies have found that when we have FACE-TO-FACE INTERACTIONS with other humans, our brains release a CHEMICAL called OXYTOCIN that BOOSTS our MOOD and can even help us LEARN and REMEMBER!

36 ONCE a week, go MEATLESS.

Raising animals for milk and meat has a really big impact on the environment. A tremendous amount of natural resources, including land, water, and energy, are used in the process. On top of that, cattle produce methane, a greenhouse gas that contributes to climate change.

So, if you feel like doing the environment a solid, make one day a week meatless. Bonus points for getting your family on board, too! It's really fun to get creative and think up delicious vegetarian meals you and your family will love.

CHEW ON THIS QUESADILLAS!

The quesadilla you order at a restaurant can be filled with lots of things, but the traditional treat from Mexico is stuffed with just one ingredient—cheese. Think of a quesadilla—or, roughly translated, "little cheesy thing" in Spanish—as a twist on a grilled cheese sandwich that you can add other ingredients to.

MAKE YOUR OWN QUESADILLAS

Get a parent's help to heat up this cheesy dish.

1. Preheat the oven to 400 degrees. In a skillet, heat 3 tablespoons of olive oil over medium heat.
2. Cut 1 zucchini in half lengthwise and thinly slice it crosswise. Add the zucchini and 1 cup of frozen corn kernels to the skillet. Cook, stirring occasionally, for 6 minutes.
3. Brush one side of 4 tortillas with olive oil. Lay 2 of the tortillas, oiled side down, on a baking sheet.
4. Place half of the vegetable filling on each tortilla, and sprinkle each with 1 cup of grated Monterey Jack cheese.
5. Place the remaining 2 tortillas on top, with their oiled side up.
6. Bake for 5 minutes, then flip. Continue baking until cheese has melted, for about 5 more minutes.
7. Cut each quesadilla into wedges and top with a handful of sliced jalapeños. Enjoy!

ZUCCHINI gets its name from the Italian word for squash.

Astronauts take TORTILLAS into space because they produce fewer crumbs than bread.

One ear of CORN produces about 600 kernels.

Eating MONTEREY JACK CHEESE may help prevent cavities.

The spicy flavor of a JALAPEÑO is concentrated near its seeds.

GRAB A PARENT AND GO ONLINE FOR OTHER RECIPES!
kids.nationalgeographic.com/kids/activities/recipes

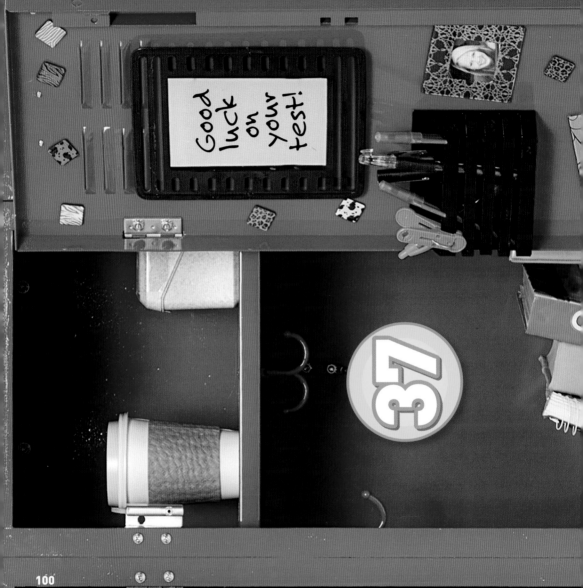

Leave a nice **note** in someone's **locker,** cubby, or mailbox.

38

CARPOOL.

Cars produce a third of the air pollution in the United States. A great way to help the environment is to reduce the number of cars on the road. To do that, walk, ride your bike, or take public transit whenever possible and, if you know someone headed to the same place as you, carpool.

FUN FACT!

In some cities, **carpooling** is **so encouraged** that they have **High Occupancy Vehicle (HOV)** lanes for cars with **two** or **more passengers.** The lanes are designed to **cut down** on your commute time—a cool **carpooling perk.**

39

Adopt YOUR PETS.

Every year, nearly eight million dogs, cats, and other animals enter animal shelters. Of these shelter animals, almost three million never find a home. But you can make a difference by steering clear of pet shops and breeders and heading to your local animal shelter to rescue a pet. Just think, you'll be a superhero to a little snugglebug hoping to find a home.

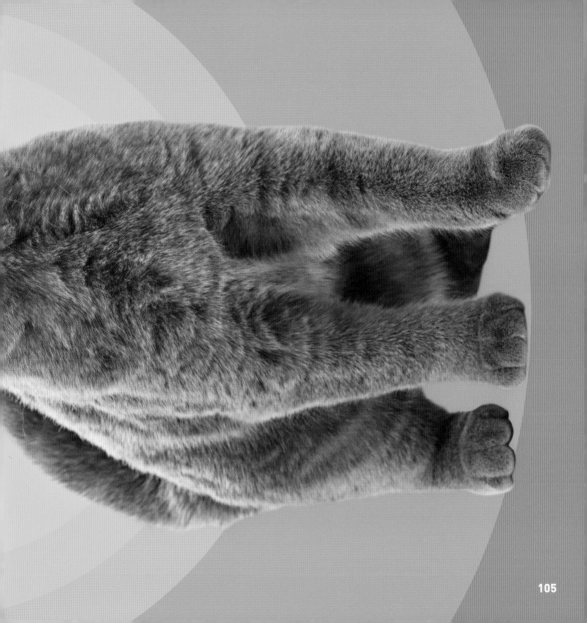

40

HOLD A CAR WASH

TO RAISE MONEY FOR A CAUSE OR CHARITY.

ASK QUESTIONS.

Think of yourself as an **investigator**—someone whose job it is to figure out **how** stuff works and **why** things are the way they are. **Always** be on the lookout for new **leads**, new **explanations**, and new **information**.

Curiosity is a seed, which when watered with **research**, blooms into **discovery**. Let yourself wonder and ask all the questions you have—like **How? Why? Who? What?**—until you find the answers you're looking for.

Bring an extra!

42

Do you need a #2 pencil for an exam? Can you get extra credit by bringing in a pack of paper towels? Are you using brown grocery bags to cover your textbooks? Were you asked to bring an empty two-liter bottle to make a cyclone in science class?

If you can, **bring an extra.**

IF SOMEONE ELSE **FORGETS**, YOU CAN **MAKE THEIR DAY** BY **GIVING THEM** ONE OF YOURS.

43

Get down with your WEiRD SELF.

Life is both too short and too long to be anything other than YOU-TO-THE-FULLEST! So what if people look when you dance in the halls? Who cares if folks do a double take at the way you style your hair?

Bring on the quirky, eccentric, wacky, bizarre, odd, peculiar, crazy, out there, zany, unusual, and weird people. Because you know what they all have in common? They're INTERESTING!

SO MUCH OF GREATNESS
IS UNIQUENESS.
GO AHEAD, BE
A LITTLE WEIRD!

Total Quotable

"Why fit in when you were born to stand out?"
—Dr. Seuss

Be Considerate.

44

Let's be honest: Nobody likes a rude person. But **minding your manners** is more than just chewing with your mouth closed and using the right fork at dinner. It's also about **considering** the people we share the world with and what makes them comfortable, both **emotionally** and **physically.**

Here are 10 of the *many* ways we can make things a bit more pleasant for one another.

1. Hold the door for people.
2. Don't let your backpack hit people in crowded places.
3. Try not to poke people with your umbrella.
4. Throw your gum away in the trash can.
5. Scooch over so someone can sit next to you on the bus.
6. Turn down your music a smidge when out in public.
7. Say "Please" and "Thank you."
8. Don't push, shove, or cut in line.
9. Watch your language—is it inclusive or offensive?
10. Let people talk without interrupting.

KEEP AT IT.

(45)

Did your cupcake pops turn out cupcake flops? That's okay, because we're going to let you in on a little secret: Everyone fails. Everyone. It's just a part of life. But the difference between the people who do great things and those who don't is that the people who do great things get back up when they fall and try again.

The famous inventor Thomas Edison said, "Many of life's failures are people who did not realize how close they were to success when they gave up." Can you imagine throwing in the towel right before you were about to find the cure for a disease or figure out how to cut greenhouse gas emissions in half or discover life on Mars?

The truth is, the only time you *really* fail is when you give up.

So, be stubborn and determined when it comes to your goals.

VOLUNTEER.

Be willing to **share your time** and **your energy** to help others. There are so **many** cool places that would be **thrilled** to have you.

10 PLACES YOU COULD LEND A HAND:

1. Retirement community
2. Animal shelter
3. After-school program for younger kids
4. Library
5. Homeless shelter
6. Children's hospital
7. Local park
8. The zoo
9. Church
10. The Red Cross

THINK before you SPEAK
(or text or tweet or leave a comment).

Have you ever noticed during big, live-televised events like awards shows, there's a delay of a couple of seconds before the program is broadcast onto people's TVs? This is to allow time for editing should someone use a swear word, have a wardrobe malfunction, or do something inappropriate. Giving yourself a similar delay is probably not a bad idea.

A slight pause gives you the chance to think about what you're going to say and how that might make others feel. Will it hurt their feelings? Will it embarrass them? Will it offend them or make them angry? Perhaps there's a more positive or productive way to say what you're thinking.

Or, maybe, if you're feeling angry and upset, it's better not to say anything at all. When you realize your intention has shifted from trying to understand someone better or being understood better to trying to hurt someone, it's probably a good idea to revisit the conversation later.

BLEEP

BLEEP

48

Embrace

people who practice **religions** *other* than **your own.**

49

Take a first aid class.

So you can be ready to help at a moment's notice.

Hope is a belief that good things will happen and that happier, better days are ahead. We need hope. **Hope** is what carries us through hard times, and it's what motivates us to work harder and be better. No matter how scary or sad or lonely things get, if you look hard enough, there is always hope. That we are stronger than we think we are. That we won't always feel the way we do now. That tomorrow is a new day. That we have no idea what the future will bring, and that it might be better than we can even dream.

"You may not always have a comfortable life and you will not always be able to solve all of the world's problems at once, but don't ever underestimate the importance you can have. History has shown us that courage can be contagious and hope can take on a life of its own." —Michelle Obama

Total Quotable

What do you hope tomorrow will be like?
What do you hope this year will be like?
What do you hope to do when you grow up?
What do you hope to accomplish?

Now, help turn your hopes into reality.
What are five things you can do to
make those hopes more likely?
What's one thing you can do today?

Learn by EXAMPLE.

51

The world is full of heroes—both big and small. Many you've heard of, but it's likely there are even more who you have not. One surefire way to get **inspired** is to learn about the people who have fought hard to improve the lives of others. Read their **biographies,** watch their **speeches** on YouTube, listen to **interviews** they've given.

Malala Yousafzai

Sally Ride

Nelson Mandela

Jackie Robinson

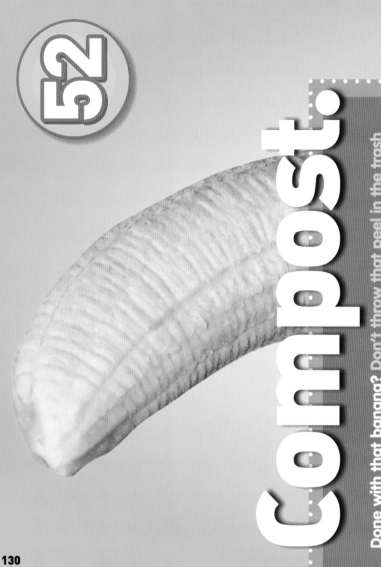

Compost.

Done with that banana? Don't throw that peel in the trash just yet! You can actually use it to make something cool. A compost pile is made up of yard trimmings, food waste, and water, which decompose and make a nutrient-rich material you can then add to the soil to help your plants grow.

Between 20 and 30 percent of what we throw away is actually COMPOSTABLE!

131

52 COMPOST.

You can easily make a compost pile outdoors in your yard, or inside using a bin. Here's how to get started composting indoors:

1. Find a container with a top (like a metal garbage bin or a plastic box).
2. Poke holes in the bottom of the container and near the top.
3. Line a tray with newspaper and put your container on the tray.
4. Add a layer of soil to the bottom of the container.
5. Next, add a layer of dry ingredients, like newspaper, twigs, dry leaves, and yard trimmings.
6. Then add your food scraps! You can add eggshells, fruit and vegetable peels, leafy greens, coffee grounds, and tea bags. (Stay away from meat, fish, and dairy, though.)
7. You want to maintain a mix of wet and dry ingredients, so when you add food scraps, also add a handful of dry ingredients.
8. Once a week, mix the compost with a scoop or trowel and add half a cup of soil.

53

Don't let where you came FROM

determine where you GO.

Where you are now in your life does not have to determine where you go, what you become, or how much you achieve. There's no doubt, some situations may make reaching your goals more difficult at times, but they most definitely do not make it impossible. Your story is just starting:

Where do you want it to go?

TALES OF TRIUMPH

Who: **Harry Reid**
Then: He was raised by a family with little money and in a house with no indoor toilet, no hot water, and no telephone.
Now: Former U.S. senator and respected congressional leader

Who: **Oprah Winfrey**
Then: She experienced tremendous personal challenges in her early life.
Now: Media maven and generous donor to many causes

Who: **Howard Schultz**
Then: He grew up in a public housing project and was the first person in his family to go to college.
Now: CEO of Starbucks and billionaire

Who: **Sonia Sotomayor**
Then: She grew up in low-income housing in Bronx, U.S.A.
Now: First Latina Supreme Court justice in the United States

54 Learn how to FIGHT *fair.*

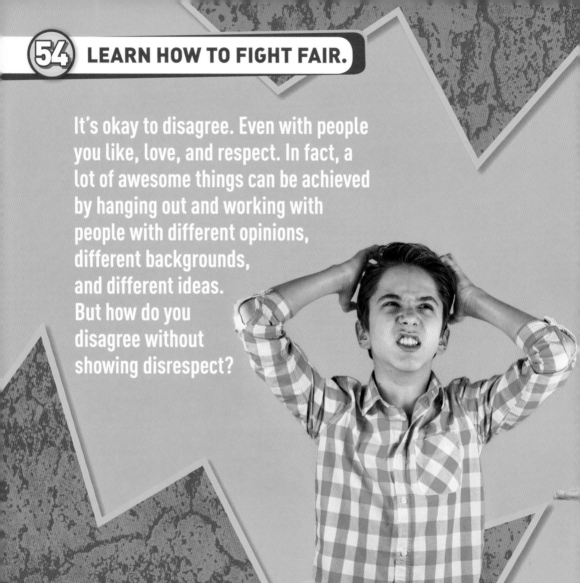

54 LEARN HOW TO FIGHT FAIR.

It's okay to disagree. Even with people you like, love, and respect. In fact, a lot of awesome things can be achieved by hanging out and working with people with different opinions, different backgrounds, and different ideas. But how do you disagree without showing disrespect?

HERE ARE SOME *tips.*

→ **NIX THE NAME-CALLING.** It just makes people defensive and shuts them down.

→ **DROP THE BLAME GAME.** Instead of saying, "You do this," or "You do that," tell someone how you feel when they act or speak a certain way. For example, "I feel really frustrated when you interrupt me."

→ **AVOID YELLING AND SHOUTING.** You're much more likely to keep things civil if you remain calm.

→ **LISTEN.** Even if you have a really good point to make, let other people finish. Give them the respect you'd like to be given.

→ **CONSIDER THEIR FEELINGS.** Think about where they're coming from and how they might be feeling.

→ **BE HONEST.**

→ **BE KIND.** No matter what someone else says to you, or what's going on around you, you can always respond with decency and respect. Don't let someone else pull you into the mud with them. As former First Lady Michelle Obama said, "When they go low, we go high."

55

PRACTICE
empathy.

If you've ever heard the expression, "Walk a mile in someone else's shoes," you've heard of empathy. Empathy is trying to understand what someone might be thinking or feeling by doing your best to understand their perspective, or where they're coming from.

By practicing empathy, you're more likely to help people in need, reduce prejudice, become kinder and more inclusive, and not be a bully. Now that's pretty powerful stuff!

Walk 56 the talk.

This is simple: Avoid saying one thing and doing another. For example, have you ever been kind to someone's face, but then talked about them behind their back? Do you know anyone who says they're a friend to the environment, but then throws gum wrappers on the ground? **If you say something, make sure your actions back it up, and vice versa.**

"Be the change that you wish to see in the world." —Mahatma Gandhi

Total Quotable

142

57 Learn about climate change.

Katharine Hayhoe is an atmospheric scientist. That means she studies what happens in the atmosphere, including weather and climate. A big part of her work is investigating how humans' impact on the atmosphere through global warming, or climate change, affects our lives and the places where we live.

Understanding climate change and what you can do about it is a really powerful way you can have an impact and make the world a better place. Katharine hosts a series of videos online called "Global Weirding," in which she answers some of the tough questions people often ask about climate change.

HERE ARE HER ANSWERS TO A FEW OF THE BIG ONES.

WHAT KEEPS OUR PLANET WARM?

Our planet has a natural blanket built into the atmosphere. This blanket is made up of heat-trapping gases, like carbon dioxide and methane, and water vapor. The sun shines down and a great deal of the sun's energy goes through that invisible blanket, to the Earth. The Earth heats up and gives off heat energy. But, just like a blanket traps our body heat on a cold night, this natural blanket traps the Earth's heat—keeping us almost 60°F (33°C) warmer than we would be otherwise. If it weren't for this amazing natural blanket, our planet would be a frozen ball of ice!

SO HOW DO HUMANS MAKE THE EARTH WARMER?

Even though the original blanket is 100 percent natural, human activities are making it thicker. By digging coal and oil and natural gas out of the ground and burning it, we are pumping massive extra amounts of carbon dioxide into the atmosphere—carbon that would otherwise stay buried in the ground for millions of years. All this extra carbon dioxide makes the blanket thicker. And what does a thicker blanket do? It traps more heat!

WHAT ARE SOME OF THE EFFECTS WE COULD SEE FROM A WARMING PLANET?

A few degrees might not sound like much, but when you're talking about the whole world, they can have a big impact.

- Climate change affects our health by causing more frequent and stronger heat waves, making air pollution worse and letting tropical diseases, and the animals and insects that carry them, spread northward as it gets warmer.

- Climate change also affects the places where we live. Hundreds of millions of people reside—and two-thirds of the world's biggest cities lie—along our coastlines, and sea level is rising. It's rising because the giant ice sheets in Greenland and Antarctica are melting and all that water is going into the oceans. Plus, warmer water takes up more space.

- Most important, though, climate change hits people even harder if they are already poor and vulnerable—and that's not fair. Nearly half of the world's population lives on just a few dollars a day. As rainfall patterns change, droughts get stronger, and heat waves get more intense, their livelihoods and very lives are at risk. When their harvests fail, they starve; when heavy downpours flood their villages, they lose their homes; and when sea level rise floods their land, they become refugees. We care about climate change because it makes poverty, hunger, and disease worse.

SO, WHAT CAN WE DO TO FIX CLIMATE CHANGE?

The first step is easy—it's figuring out how big your carbon footprint is. Your carbon footprint is the amount of carbon dioxide that's emitted because of your personal actions and behaviors (like using air-conditioning, eating meat, flying on airplanes, etc.). The average American emits about 18 tons (16 t) of carbon dioxide into the atmosphere each year. That's four times the global average. You can determine what your carbon footprint is by searching for a "carbon calculator" online. There you'll see what parts of your lifestyle are contributing most to your footprint and what are the smartest changes you can make to reduce it.

WHAT KINDS OF CHANGES ARE WE TALKING ABOUT?

- Some are small: like recycling, washing your clothes in cold water instead of hot water (which uses five times the energy), or swapping old incandescent lightbulbs for more efficient LEDs.
- You could help your parents make heating and cooling your home more efficient by caulking your leaky windows and adding insulation to your attic.
- There's a lot we can do in our own diets, too, like eating locally produced foods, not wasting foods, opting for tap water over bottled water, and eating lower in the food chain (that means more veggies and less meat). One pound of red meat creates about 18 times the amount of emissions as a vegetarian meal!
- Also, look at the way you commute to school or work. Consider carpooling—even once a week would help—or walking or riding your bike. A full quarter of the average American's emissions come from driving!

DO IT TODAY!

Our personal choices control only about 40 percent of national emissions. In reality, the government also must act. That's why one of the most important things each of us can do is let our elected officials—in city hall, at the state capitol, or in Washington, D.C.—know that we are concerned about climate change and we want them to address it. Grab a parent and visit *house.gov* and *senate.gov* to find out who your representatives are and call or write them a letter today!

DONATE your old toys and stuffed animals

58

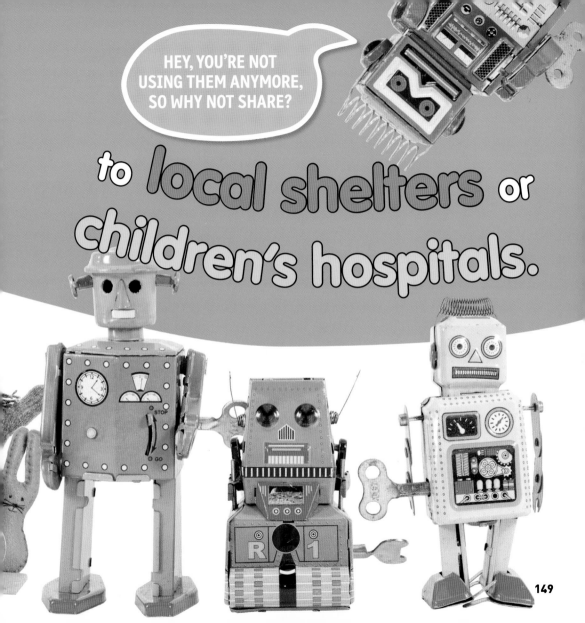

Be passionate.

59

Bindi Sue Irwin calls herself a wildlife warrior, a term her father, conservationist Steve Irwin (known to many as "The Crocodile Hunter") coined. "A wildlife warrior is someone who stands up and speaks for those who cannot speak for themselves," says Bindi. "I work every day to try to encourage others to get involved and to want to make a difference in our world."

Bindi is a passionate wildlife conservationist, and she works with her family at the Australia Zoo, which her grandparents opened in 1970, and at the family's nonprofit organization. The organization, Wildlife Warriors, helps protect orangutans and tigers in Sumatra, cheetahs in South Africa, Asian elephants in Cambodia, and rhinos in Kenya, among other things.

When did you discover you had a passion for wildlife conservation?

Love for wildlife and wild places has been in my blood since birth. Since I can remember, I have wanted to be just like my parents and carry on all the extraordinary wildlife conservation work that they started. I live right in the middle of Australia Zoo, which means that every day brings a new and different wildlife adventure. We have more than 1,200 gorgeous animals at Australia Zoo, and we are the most hands-on zoological facility in the world. You can cuddle koalas, kiss rhinos, scratch Komodo dragons, feed lemurs, hold birds and snakes—you name it! My dad, Steve Irwin, often said, "People want to save things that they love." By giving our visitors the chance to interact with our beautiful animals and knowledgeable staff, we have the chance to educate and inspire.

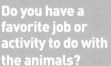

Do you have a favorite animal to work with these days?

Living at Australia Zoo, I am surrounded by so many beautiful creatures. Crocodiles and snakes are two of my favorites; however, I think that my all-time favorite animal would have to be the echidna. They are so sweet and rather unusual looking! They share a similarity with the platypus, as they are both monotremes, which means that they are egg-laying mammals. They are such funny little creatures, and being covered in spikes, they kind of look like walking pincushions!

Do you have a favorite job or activity to do with the animals?

I really love spending time with all our gorgeous animals. Often at the end of a busy day at Australia Zoo, when everyone has left for the day, I will go and just sit on the grass in our giant kangaroo paddock and spend time with the roos, watching the sun set. I find that I'm most at peace being around wildlife; it seems to be the greatest form of meditation!

Is there anything you've learned through your work that you apply to the rest of your life?

My dad always taught me that we must treat animals the way we wish to be treated. I think that his advice applies to both animals and people. In order to protect our planet, we must first learn to be kind in every part of life. If we show kindness for and to each other, we can be kind to our wildlife and, in turn, our planet.

What fuels your passion for wildlife?

I want to make the world a better place for the next generations. I want to ensure that we always have clean air, fresh drinking water, and an abundance of wildlife, forever. I think that it is extraordinary how every animal has a real personality and special importance on the planet. It has always amazed me how connected we all are and that the footprints we leave on Earth today will have an impact on wildlife and wild places far into the future. Every time we lose an animal species, it's like losing a brick from the house; eventually the house just collapses.

What's something that you're working on now that you're excited about?

There is one conservation project that wins for most thrilling! On our annual crocodile research trip, in Far North Queensland, we catch crocs to track and learn more about them, in order to protect them. Our Australia Zoo team works with the University of Queensland to create the world's most extensive research study. We are not only rewriting university textbooks with our groundbreaking research on saltwater crocodiles, we are also able to help more people live safely throughout crocodile territory and understand the behavior of crocodiles. We are currently tracking 150 crocodiles in the Wenlock River, along the Steve Irwin Wildlife Reserve. I think the best part of the trip is spending a month camping in the bush with family and friends, doing life-changing croc research. It's such a fun time sitting around campfires, working with crocs, sleeping under the stars and being so far away from any towns or cities.

Do you remember a time when maybe things weren't going as planned, but your passion for the project fueled you to keep going?

When your passion in life is conservation and trying to spread love and light, sometimes it can be challenging to remain positive. There are so many issues facing our world today that it can seem a little daunting at times. However, you must find the strength within yourself to make a difference and keep moving forward, especially as a young person. My best advice to all young people who wish to make a difference in the world is to follow your dreams no matter what. You must surround yourself with all the support and love from family and friends to keep you going. And above all, you should remember that no matter what happens in life, it is so important to follow your heart.

153

60 CONSIDER DONATING YOUR HAIR.

THERE ARE SEVERAL ORGANIZATIONS THAT CREATE **HAIRPIECES** AND **WIGS** FROM **DONATED HAIR.** THESE ARE THEN **GIVEN** TO PEOPLE EXPERIENCING **HAIR LOSS** FOR A **MEDICAL REASON,** LIKE A DISEASE CALLED **ALOPECIA** OR NEEDING TO UNDERGO **CHEMOTHERAPY TREATMENTS** FOR CANCER, AND WHO MIGHT NOT BE ABLE TO AFFORD THEM OTHERWISE.

Use *REUSABLE* WATER BOTTLES.

Think about how many bottles of water you drink in a day: Maybe you grab one for the bus to school, drink another for lunch, another to beat the afternoon slump, and maybe even two or three during soccer practice. That adds up quickly! If this describes you, you're not alone. Each year, Americans buy more than 29 billion bottles of water—more than any other country in the world. To make all those bottles, more than 17 million barrels of oil are used. That's enough to keep a million cars going for 12 months!

HOW CAN YOU HELP? Simple, grab a REUSABLE PLASTIC OR GLASS BOTTLE. You're saving the planet, and there's a bonus: They come in superfun designs!

START A CLUB.

62

GET **TOGETHER** WITH OTHER **PEOPLE** WHO WANT TO **DO GOOD** IN YOUR **NEIGHBORHOOD.**

Walk to fight disease

There are LOTS of WALKS and RUNS that raise money for local and national charities. It's a FUN WAY to spend a day with friends, family, and people in your community and get some FRESH AIR and EXERCISE—and you usually get a cool T-shirt to remind you of the FUN YOU HAD.

or support a cause.

64 Study SCIENCE.

MAANASA MENDU, 15, is proof that you're never too young to change the world. She won the Discovery Education 3M Young Scientist Challenge with her invention, called **HARVEST**, which creates renewable energy from sunlight, wind, and precipitation.

When did you become interested in science?

In elementary school, I actually loved math. Then in middle school, I had amazing STEM [science, technology, engineering, and mathematics] teachers who used demonstrations, interesting facts, and humor to really push science beyond the limits of the classroom. Also, through competitions like Science Olympiad, I realized science includes everything from crazy questions to the future of our world!

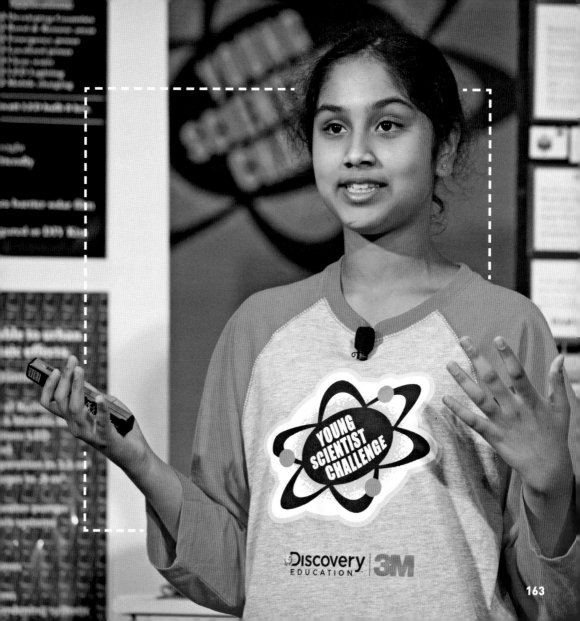

64) STUDY SCIENCE.

What inspired you to create HARVEST?

Every summer my family visits India, and there I experienced persistent blackouts. This meant no lighting or air-conditioning for my family. But for over one-fifth of the global population, darkness remains a permanent reality. While observing the swaying of tree branches, I realized they resembled how piezoelectric materials produce electricity when exposed to the wind. Electricity is fundamental to modern society, and providing a sustainable source of electricity to our entire world should be a top priority. So, I decided to create a device that mimics the motion of trees to produce electricity.

Can you talk a little bit about how it works and how you see it being used?

HARVEST is a bio-inspired device that harvests mechanical energy in the forms of wind and precipitation through the piezoelectric effect—an amazing phenomena in which certain

materials produce electricity when exposed to mechanical strain (when force is applied to a material causing it to change shape or bend)—and solar energy in a single design. HARVEST can be applied to harvest the unused potential of wind energy in urban areas or to provide a stable source of power for basic necessities in rural and remote areas or in developing countries.

Did you learn anything about yourself in this process?

Yes, I had no idea that I could be so persistent and hardworking for a single project! I really did gain a lot of self-satisfaction and confidence between coming up with the initial idea to building a complete prototype.

Whom in your life do you like to discuss science topics and ideas with?

My dad Sreepathi, mom Padmaja, sister Haasini, and close friends. I love all the different perspectives they offer! I also like to record my ideas and thoughts in a journal.

What are you working on now?

My goal now is to deploy HARVEST across the world to provide a stable and sustainable source of power for basic necessities in developing countries. First, I need to maximize the efficiency of my product by testing different materials and configurations. Then I plan to conduct practicality testing to determine any further environmental implications. Finally, I plan on reaching out to businesses and nonprofit organizations to deploy my innovation across the world!

Do you have any advice for other young people interested in science?

My biggest piece of advice is to try stuff, and, ultimately, believe in yourself! Even though an idea may seem crazy, you may never know its potential unless you try. Remember to take risks! If you have an idea or a problem to solve, don't hesitate to sketch out a model or build a prototype just using common household materials. When people don't believe in you, or even when you don't believe in yourself, you must be brave and go for it. You'll be surprised at what you can accomplish when you put your fears aside. Everyone has the potential to change the world for the better, and the hard part is they just have to harness it!

65 Pick up trash

Do you have a favorite place to spend time in nature? Get some of your friends and family together and spend a weekend morning there, getting rid of garbage and sprucing it up.

66 *Learn how to* *SIMMER DOWN.*

Have you ever gotten so **MAD** or so **FRUSTRATED** that you couldn't think straight? Or felt like your face was about to **BURST INTO FLAMES**? That's because when you get angry, your brain begins sending signals to your body to **REV THINGS UP**. But if you've ever said something you **TOTALLY REGRETTED** (at least, once you calmed down), you know reacting in the heat of the moment isn't the best idea. Learning how to **DE-ESCALATE** (a fancy word for calm down) is one of the keys to making the world a **BETTER PLACE**. If you can keep yourself from getting **TOO HEATED**, your relationships will **IMPROVE**, you'll get into **FEWER ARGUMENTS**, and you'll be able to talk through tough things **WITHOUT** feeling like your head's going to **POP OFF**.

66 LEARN HOW TO SIMMER DOWN.

Here, Susan Kaiser Greenland, author of *Mindful Games* and a mindfulness and meditation teacher, explains just how one might do that.

What is mindful awareness?
It's when we keep our mind focused on a chosen object, and don't get lost in distraction. When we are mindful, we have a heightened awareness of what's going on in the mind—like what we see, hear, taste, smell, feel, think, or intuit—and we can notice our current state of mind (*Am I agitated? Dull? Alert? Distracted?*).

How can practicing mindful awareness help when you're feeling angry or stressed or wound up?
When we feel angry, stressed, or wound up, our nervous system moves into a less flexible, more reactive mode where it's difficult—if not impossible—to learn, to listen, to respond thoughtfully, or to be open-minded. When we practice mindfulness, we're better able to catch ourselves before those emotions kick into high gear. If we catch ourselves soon enough, we can reverse course.

What's something someone can do to help calm down in a moment of intense emotion?
First, just notice that the strong feelings are starting to take over or have taken over. Then move your attention away from thinking about the emotion, or what caused the emotion, or your worries, toward something you're experiencing in the present moment. This could be a sensation in your body, like how your breathing feels; the sensation of taking each step while walking slowly and silently; the sounds in the room; a word, like counting or a mantra; or a present-moment task, like rubbing a worry stone, squeezing a stress ball, playing the piano, or gardening.

How might doing this make the world a better place?
If you can catch yourself before your emotions get too heightened, and reverse these feelings, you are likely to be less reactive, more open to new ideas, more able to listen, and, hopefully, kinder and more compassionate.

If we see that someone else is in a reactive, inflexible frame, it's important to remember that engaging with them then is probably going to escalate rather than de-escalate the conflict. So, it's a good idea to wait before reengaging. You might change the subject, laugh, joke—do anything to give the other person enough breathing room so that they can settle down.

67

Try to include 🧍🧍🧍🧍🧍 EVERYONE.

EVERYONE has been left out at some point or another. And **EVERYONE** knows how **AWFUL** it feels. So, whenever possible, **EXTEND THE INVITE!** It's kind, it's the **RIGHT** thing to do, and you'll soon discover that the old expression is right: **THE MORE, THE MERRIER.**

FUN FACT!

NATALIE HAMPTON, a 16-year-old from California, U.S.A., **DEVELOPED AN APP** called Sit With Us that helps students find friendly folks to **SIT WITH** in their school cafeteria.

GET ACTIVE IN YOUR COMMUNITY.

68

Want to make the world a better place? Start close to home. It's easy to see differences you can make from where you are; after all, you know your own community best. Does your neighborhood need recycling bins? Lights on the basketball court? A community garden? Come up with a list, then brainstorm with a trusted adult which item you can tackle first, and how.

69

Forgive SOMEONE.

"It is one of the greatest gifts you can give yourself, to forgive. Forgive everybody."
—Maya Angelou

Total Quotable

Get to know your NEIGHBORS.

(Then think of ways you can help them.)

Whether it's raking leaves, shoveling snow, or bringing in their garbage cans, one of the upsides to being part of a community is that you can watch out for one another.

70

Shovel snow.

Do something nice for your neighbors!

Bring in garbage cans.

Rake leaves.

Fix

something.

**A leaky faucet...
a hole in your jeans...
a frayed basketball net.**

Find something that is **old, broken,** or **needs an upgrade**—and **fix it**. To figure out **how,** you may need to enlist the **help** of a **parent** or other **adult, consult the Internet,** or **visit a hardware store** and **ask for some advice.** But be warned, the **serious self-satisfaction** from getting your hands dirty is **addictive!**

Give people a chance.

Very nearly 100 percent of our DNA is the same as that of all other humans. Next time you meet someone new and feel yourself beginning to judge them because of things you think make you different, be open-minded instead, give them a chance, and get to know who they really are.

72

73

Spread the ♥ LOVE

Hug a friend. Leave your parents a **thank-you** note. Tell your sister—gasp!—you *love* her. When you're feeling good feelings, express them.

74

SMILE

Want to brighten up a room, ease some tension, and put some positive energy into the world? Then go ahead, show 'em your pearly whites! The wider the grin, the better.

Total Quotable

"Let us always meet each other with a smile, for the smile is the beginning of love."
—Mother Teresa

75

PRACTICE
SPEAKING IN
PUBLIC.

YOUR **FAMILY** AND YOUR **FRIENDS,** YOUR **CLASSMATES,** AND YOUR **COMMUNITY** ALL NEED TO HEAR YOUR **GREAT STORIES** AND **IDEAS.** SO PRACTICE TALKING IN FRONT OF PEOPLE AS MUCH AS YOU CAN. THE **MORE** YOU DO IT, THE **MORE COMFORTABLE YOU'LL FEEL.**

76

Think OUTSIDE the box.

When looking for ways to make the world a better place, don't limit yourself to what's already been done. Forge your own path, do your own thing, go where no one has ever gone before.

Total Quotable

"If we keep doing what we're doing, we're going to keep getting what we're getting."
—Stephen Covey

77

CELEBRATE
others' success.

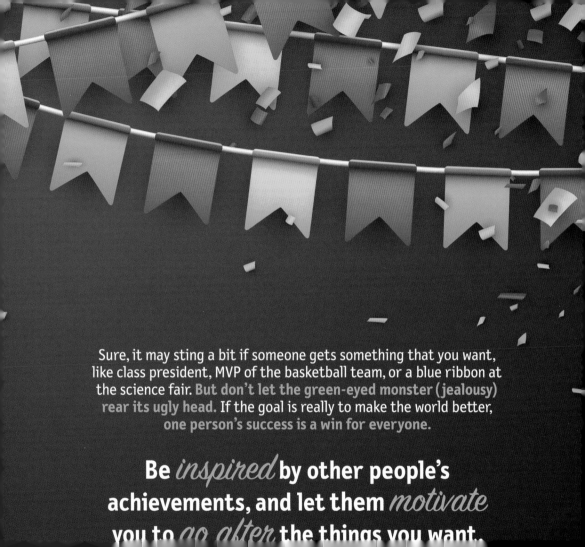

Sure, it may sting a bit if someone gets something that you want, like class president, MVP of the basketball team, or a blue ribbon at the science fair. But don't let the green-eyed monster (jealousy) rear its ugly head. If the goal is really to make the world better, one person's success is a win for everyone.

Be *inspired* by other people's achievements, and let them *motivate* you to *go after* the things you want.

There will be times in your life when you look around and see things you think should be different, or situations you think should be better. And sometimes, the best person to lead the charge for change is none other than YOU. It's in these moments that you will need to rise to the challenge and lead the way. As President Barack Obama said, "Change will not come if we wait for some other person or some other time. We are the ones we've been waiting for. We are the change that we seek."

MEET SAFAATH AHMED ZAHIR, 26,

a Young Leader for the Sustainable Development Goals recognized by the UN Secretary-General's Envoy on Youth. She grew up in Malé, the capital city of the Republic of Maldives, a South Asian country made up of islands in the Indian Ocean. She is a leading women's rights advocate and is dedicated to getting more women into leadership positions, as well as empowering women economically, in her country.

WAY. ⟶

What made you decide that you wanted to do something to help with gender equality?

Honestly, it came from the utter frustration of having to deal with daily sexism. I went to college in Malaysia, and then I got my master's in finance at a university in China. When I returned home to the Maldives, I felt responsible for my community. Then I met a group of dynamic ladies who founded a nonprofit called Women On Boards, which aims to increase female representation on corporate boards. This idea really motivated me for so many reasons—it felt so personal. WOB's work has enabled broader female participation in the economy throughout the country.

How has Women On Boards changed things in the Maldives?

We have greatly influenced both businesses and the government to encourage more female participation in the country's economy. Interestingly—or sadly, rather—the issue of underrepresentation of women in leadership was less spoken of before WOB. Our awareness events have helped many to gain confidence in women.

Who are your role models? Who inspires you to be a leader for positive change?

I'm always inspired by my family! Having said that, I've long admired Margaret Thatcher and President Mohamed Nasheed—the first democratically elected president in the Maldives, he served from 2008 to 2012—both of whom made the impossible possible. It was 1979 when Ms. Thatcher got elected as the first female prime minister of the UK. Did you know that even she doubted whether there would ever be a female prime minister in her lifetime? Today, more than 45 years since Thatcher got elected, electing a female leader still seems impossible in even the world's strongest economies, let alone my own nation.

President Nasheed has inspired me ever since I was a teenager, because he literally founded our Maldivian democracy. He is an inspiration to every young Maldivian who dares to make a difference, because he dared to make that difference!

What would you like to achieve through your current work? What are your goals?

Whether it is creating awareness, or connecting young people with opportunities, I always openly advocate for women in leadership. Democracy holds a very special place in my heart, and I am passionate about the development of free and democratic societies. I passionately believe that democracy empowers people. It empowers me to be a good leader and to stand up for what's right! I care about free speech; I care about voting to express my passion; and I care about having a greater stake in the development and peace of my own community.

What advice would you give to young people who want to make a difference?

My biggest piece of advice is know that you have a great stake in making things happen for your community. You are the future. We can only evolve toward the right path with your engagement. You are absolutely pivotal. Don't be afraid to get into policymaking or anything you dream of. Chase your beautiful dreams, and for sure they will add value to our world.

Take yourself SERIOUSLY.

You are capable of doing great things, right now, wherever you are. Don't underestimate the difference you can make in your community, your country, or in the lives of people you meet.

"No matter what people tell you, words and ideas can change the world."
—Robin Williams

But also *DON'T* take yourself *TOO* SERIOUSLY.

Have you ever mispronounced a word, had broccoli stuck in your braces, or shown up to school with your zipper down? Super embarrassing, right? But definitely not the end of the world. Don't let an awkward moment keep you from putting yourself out there again. When you learn to give yourself a break and be okay with not being perfect, you'll have an easier time extending that compassion to other people as well.

"Don't be looking for perfection. Don't be short-tempered with yourself. And you'll be a whole lot nicer to be around with everyone else."
—Mary Tyler Moore

Total Quotable

201

Be on the lookout for BULLYING.

81

BE ON THE LOOKOUT FOR BULLYING.

If you see someone being bullied, you can be more than a bystander. **Standing up for other people is a r**[...] **powerful way to make a difference.** Here are fi[...] **ways** to do that, according to StopBullying.gov:

1. Be their friend.
Call them after school, send them a text message, or invite them to be your lab partner in science class. Just be nice to them so that they know they're not alone.

2. Tell a trusted adult.
Talk to someone you feel comfortable with and who listens to you as soon as possible. Don't keep what you saw a secret, definitely reach out to someone else who can help.

3. Help them get away.
If someone's being bullied, you can he[...] by giving them a chance to get away [...] the person who is bullying. It can be as simple as inviting them to come play soccer with you at recess, walking with them to class, or inviting them to sit with you and your friends on the bus.

4. Set a good example.
Let people know you're against bullying. Make posters, start an anti-bullying club, and don't gossip or make fun of people. Include students who have been bullied or reach out to people who sometimes get left out.

5. Don't give bullying an audience.
Often, people who bully get revved up and encouraged by people watching, cheering, or laughing. So, to let people know you're against bullying, don't laugh or agree with the person who is bullying. You might even look or walk away. Then definitely try one or more of the first four steps to help make the situation better.

What counts as BULLYING?

When someone **repeatedly** teases someone, threatens them, insults them, physically hurts them, or excludes them.

"Disrespect invites disrespect. Violence incites violence. When the powerful use their position to bully, we all lose."
—Meryl Streep

MAKE and/or appreciate

82

Have you ever looked at a painting, watched a movie, or listened to a song and felt awe, joy, fear, anger, sadness, or humor? Art has a way of teaching us new things and introducing us to new ideas by making us feel. By making art, you're sharing your life experiences, your perspective, and your hopes, dreams, and fears with other people.

NEED SOME INSPIRATION?

Draw a line down the middle of a poster board. On the left side, glue, tape, write, or draw words and images that express a problem you see with the world today. On the right side, put words and images that represent what you think is the solution.

66 Total Quotable 99

"If art is to nourish the roots of our culture, society must set the artist free to follow his vision wherever it takes him."
—John F. Kennedy

PLAY!

Think you're **too old** for a good ol' fashioned game of hide-and-seek? **Think again!** Playing is **good** for **you!** It encourages creativity and imagination, gets you moving and socializing—and it's **FUN!** All of those are things that will help **make the world a better place** for you and the people around you.

83

84

Gossip less (or not at all).

It can feel fun to listen to, or even spread, a juicy story about someone. But afterward, there's the inevitable pang of guilt. After all, you'd be pretty bummed if people were talking that way about you. Challenge: Try not to gossip for a whole week and see how you feel. It definitely requires discipline, but chances are, you'll feel proud of yourself.

Total Quotable

"Strong minds discuss ideas, average minds discuss events, weak minds discuss people."
—Socrates

211

85

Celebrate your
BIRTHDAY
by buying a gift and
DONATING it to a local HOMELESS
or WOMEN'S SHELTER.

GIFT CARD
$10
$10

GIFT CARD
$15
$15

86

Take part in POLITICS.

You may not be old enough to vote **yet,** but that **doesn't mean** you can't start caring about **who is running your country.** Pay attention to what's going on. Politicians make a lot of decisions that affect **your life** and the lives of **people around you.** If you have ideas or concerns, **attend local government meetings, create a petition, write letters to political leaders,** or find other ways to **make your voice heard.**

Say Hello and Thank You

From the bus driver to the librarian, don't forget to let people know that you appreciate the hard work they put in to make your life easier. Eye contact and a simple greeting let people know you notice, and it goes a long way.

78

Read, read, read!

Think of books as candy for your brain. The more you know, the more you can put your smarts to use to help others!

89

DON'T PUSH people's BUTTONS on *purpose.*

You know that thing that drives your brother or sister crazy? Like biting your nails or humming in the car or leaving your jacket on the couch? Try not to do it, even if it's just for one day.

90

Be KIND to ANIMALS.

Feel all the feels.

91

224

Have you ever felt silly for getting so worked up about something? Sure, you may have just been having a bad day or feeling overwhelmed. But maybe, just maybe, it was something else. Maybe you were having **a strong emotional reaction** because you **care a lot.** And caring a lot is not a bad thing. Caring a lot is actually the only way change happens and good things get done. **So let yourself care,** even if sometimes, it seems like you're the only one who does.

92 Try to go **24 HourS** without complaining.

Give it a try!
Make an effort to be extra patient with **yourself** and **others**.

93

DONATE to a food pantry.

Raid your kitchen cabinets and then **ASK** if you can put out a box for donations by your school's front office. **Be sure to** collect items with a LONG SHELF LIFE, like CANNED FOODS, peanut butter, pasta, and boxed snacks and cereal.

94

RETURN

YOUR SHOPPING CART TO THE CART CORRAL.

Someone has to put those back, you know.

Cheer someone up.

95

95 CHEER SOMEONE UP.

Here are 10 ways to brighten someone's day.

1. Make them a **mixed CD** or a Spotify **playlist.**

4. BAKE them a **treat,** or buy them one from the vending machine.

2. Listen—and **let them vent** if they need to.

3. Find a **fun picture** of the two of you, then make and decorate a picture frame out of wooden craft sticks.

234

5. Make them a **homemade** greeting card.

6. **Remind them** of something they have to **look forward to,** like the weekend!

9. Pick them a **flower**—just **not** from their front yard.

10. Lend them **a book or comic book** that you like to read.

7. **Write** them a **funny** poem. **Laughter** is the **best** medicine after all.

8. Go for a **walk** together after school, play some basketball, or have a **dance party!**

96 Accept Compliments.

Let yourself feel **happy** that someone paid you a compliment, is being nice, and is pointing out something **positive** about you or your work. **Not only is it good for your self-esteem, it will make them feel good, too!**

97

Be the kind of *friend* you'd like to *have.*

make **PET BEDS** for **ANIMAL** SHELTERS.

98

98 MAKE PET BEDS FOR ANIMAL SHELTERS.

GIVE YOUR LOCAL SHELTER A CALL TO SEE IF IT IS IN NEED OF PET BEDS and if so, if the shelter wants them to be a certain size to fit its cages. Then get crafting for a good cause.

Figure out what size bed you would like to make. Then add eight inches (20 cm) to the length and eight inches to the width and cut two pieces of fabric that size.

Stack the two pieces of fabric on top of each other and cut strips one inch (2.5 cm) wide by four inches (10 cm) long along the four sides of the fabric.

Tie the two pieces of fabric together by tying knots in the corresponding strips. But leave a few consecutive strips untied where you'll stuff the cushion.

Use stuffing from a fabric store—or old pieces of cloth or clothing or old pillows—to stuff the bed.

Tie the remaining strips together and voilà! A comfy cushion for a pet in need.

99

PAY ATTENTION.

244

There are **TONS** of opportunities **EVERY DAY** to make the world a **BIT BETTER,** but you have to be **PRESENT, HAVE YOUR EYES AND EARS OPEN,** and be **PAYING ATTENTION** to what's going on.

Whether it's **READING THE NEWSPAPER** to catch up on current events or **LOOKING UP FROM YOUR PHONE** to notice someone who needs a seat on the bus, you should **ALWAYS** be on the lookout for **WAYS TO HELP.**

Celebrate
every day!

100

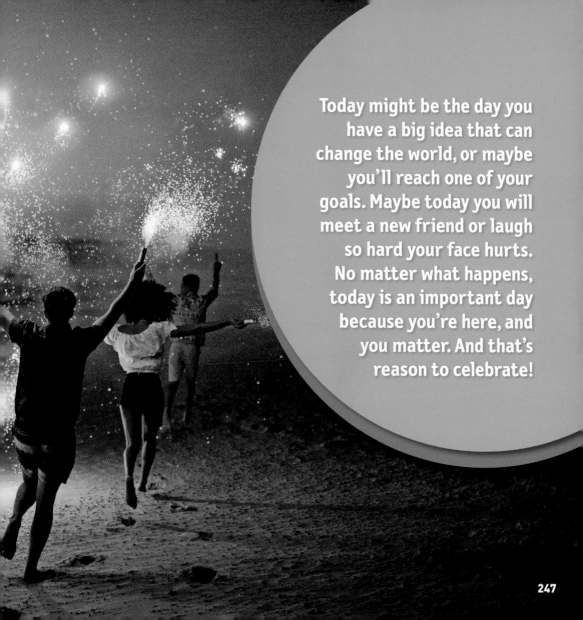

Today might be the day you have a big idea that can change the world, or maybe you'll reach one of your goals. Maybe today you will meet a new friend or laugh so hard your face hurts. No matter what happens, today is an important day because you're here, and you matter. And that's reason to celebrate!

WAYS TO MAKE THE WORLD A BETTER PLACE

Here's a quick list of all the awesome ways you can make the world better featured in this book. This list is by no means comprehensive. There are so many creative actions—big and small—you can do to make someone's day, help the planet, and have a positive impact. But if you habitually strive to do the things on this list, you're off to a great start! So what are you waiting for? Go on and make the world a better place!

1. Be open to different opinions.
2. Find your voice and raise it.
3. Study history.
4. Spend time with older individuals.
5. Recycle.
6. Stand up for justice.
7. Be nice to yourself.
8. Don't be a water waster.
9. Dream big.
10. Practice positive body image.
11. Don't let your fears hold you back.
12. Have FUN!
13. Think about things critically.
14. Turn off the lights when you leave the room.
15. Help someone out.
16. Practice gratitude.
17. Trust your intuition.
18. Get to know YOU!
19. Take action.
20. Listen.
21. Think globally.
22. Let your trash be someone else's treasure.
23. Take up a collection.
24. Be a welcoming committee!
25. Write a thank-you note to someone who's not expecting it.
26. Notice something that needs to be taken care of, and do it before you're asked.
27. Spend time reading with someone younger.
28. Be generous with compliments.
29. Plant a tree.
30. Join a team.
31. Learn another language.
32. Own up to your mistakes.
33. Put your talents to use.
34. Teach someone how to do something you know how to do well.
35. Disconnect from your electronics.
36. Once a week, go meatless.
37. Leave a nice note in someone's locker, cubby, or mailbox.
38. Carpool.
39. Adopt your pets.
40. Hold a car wash to raise money for a cause or charity.
41. Ask questions.

42. Bring an extra!
43. Get down with your weird self.
44. Be considerate.
45. Keep at it.
46. Volunteer.
47. Think before you speak (or text or tweet or leave a comment).
48. Embrace people who practice religions other than your own.
49. Take a first aid class.
50. Hope.
51. Learn by example.
52. Compost.
53. Don't let where you came from determine where you go.
54. Learn how to fight fair.
55. Practice empathy.
56. Walk the talk.
57. Learn about climate change.
58. Donate your old toys and stuffed animals to local shelters or children's hospitals.
59. Be passionate.
60. Consider donating your hair.
61. Use reusable water bottles.
62. Start a club.
63. Walk to fight disease or support a cause.
64. Study science.
65. Pick up trash.
66. Learn how to simmer down.
67. Try to include everyone.
68. Get active in your community.
69. Forgive someone.
70. Get to know your neighbors.
71. Fix something.
72. Give people a chance.
73. Spread the love.
74. Smile.
75. Practice speaking in public.
76. Think outside the box.
77. Celebrate others' success.
78. Lead the way.
79. Take yourself seriously.
80. But also don't take yourself *too* seriously.
81. Be on the lookout for bullying.
82. Make and/or appreciate art.
83. Play!
84. Gossip less (or not at all).
85. Celebrate your birthday by buying a gift and donating it to a local homeless or women's shelter.
86. Take part in politics.
87. Say "Hello" and "Thank you."
88. Read, read, read!
89. Don't push people's buttons on purpose.
90. Be kind to animals.
91. Feel all the feels.
92. Try to go 24 hours without complaining.
93. Donate to a food pantry.
94. Return your shopping cart to the cart corral.
95. Cheer someone up.
96. Accept compliments.
97. Be the kind of friend you'd like to have.
98. Make pet beds for animal shelters.
99. Pay attention.
100. Celebrate every day!

INDEX

Boldface indicates illustrations.
If illustrations are included within
a page span, the entire span is
boldface.

INDEX

Find Out More

Grab a parent and visit these websites for more information!

1. nationalgeographic.com/explorers
2. firstbook.org
3. kids.nationalgeographic.com
4. events.nationalgeographic.com
5. volunteermatch.org

PHOTO CREDITS

For Abby, Andy, and Jackson,
who make my world infinitely better.
—LMG

Since 1888, the National Geographic Society has funded more than 12,000 research, exploration, and preservation projects around the world. The Society receives funds from National Geographic Partners, LLC, funded in part by your purchase. A portion of the proceeds from this book supports this vital work. To learn more, visit natgeo.com/info.

NATIONAL GEOGRAPHIC and Yellow Border Design are trademarks of the National Geographic Society, used under license.

For more information, visit nationalgeographic.com, call 1-800-647-5463, or write to the following address:

National Geographic Partners
1145 17th Street N.W.
Washington, D.C. 20036-4688 U.S.A.

Visit us online at nationalgeographic.com/books

For librarians and teachers: ngchildrensbooks.org

More for kids from National Geographic:
kids.nationalgeographic.com

For information about special discounts for bulk purchases, please contact National Geographic Books Special Sales: specialsales@natgeo.com

For rights or permissions inquiries, please contact National Geographic Books Subsidiary Rights: bookrights@natgeo.com

Trade paperback ISBN: 978-1-4263-2997-5
Reinforced library binding ISBN: 978-1-4263-2998-2

Designed by Rosie Gowsell-Pattison

The publisher would like to thank the team who helped make this book possible: Ariane Szu-Tu, associate editor; Hillary Leo, photo editor; Lori Epstein, photo director; Callie Broaddus, senior designer; Becky Baines, executive editor; Joan Gossett, editorial production manager; and Gus Tello and Anne LeongSon, design production assistants.

Printed in China
17/PPS/1